1 MONTH OF
FREE
READING

at

www.ForgottenBooks.com

By purchasing this book you are eligible for one month membership to ForgottenBooks.com, giving you unlimited access to our entire collection of over 1,000,000 titles via our web site and mobile apps.

To claim your free month visit:

www.forgottenbooks.com/free715756

ISBN 978-0-656-26277-9
PIBN 10715756

This book is a reproduction of an important historical work. Forgotten Books uses
state-of-the-art technology to digitally reconstruct the work, preserving the original format
whilst repairing imperfections present in the aged copy. In rare cases, an imperfection in
the original, such as a blemish or missing page, may be replicated in our edition. We do,
however, repair the vast majority of imperfections successfully; any imperfections that
remain are intentionally left to preserve the state of such historical works.

ANNUAL REPORT

OF THE

TOWN OFFICERS

OF THE

TOWN OF ASHLAND

FOR THE

Year Ending February 15, 1917

1917

Record Print, Plymouth.

71.7

WARRANT.

To the Inhabitants of the Town of Ashland, in the County of Grafton, in said State, qualified to vote in Town Affairs:

You are hereby notified to meet at the Town Hall in said Ashland on Tuesday, the thirteenth day of March, 1917, at nine of the clock in the forenoon to act upon the following subjects:

1. To choose all necessary town officers for the year ensuing.

2. To raise such sums of money as may be necessary to defray town charges for the ensuing year, and make appropriation of the same.

3. To see how much money the town will vote to raise and appropriate for the increase and support of the town library.

4. To see how much money the town will vote to raise and appropriate for the observance of Memorial day.

5. To see how much money the town will vote to raise and appropriate for the laying out, building and repairing of highways and bridges for the ensuing year.

6. To see how much money the town will vote to raise and appropriate to defray the current expenses of the fire department for the ensuing year.

7. To see how much money the town will vote to raise and appropriate to defray the expenses of the town poor.

8. To see if the town will vote to repair the concrete streets and sidewalks and raise and appropriate money for the same.

9. To see if the town will vote to install three street lights on Collins street, leading by the residence of Almon Carter, Charles B. Huckins and the leatherboard mill.

10. To see if the town will vote to widen the bridge on Main street near Fifield's Garage, over Squam river, and appropriate money for the same.

11. To see if the town will vote to build a concrete street on Winter street, from near the residence of John Morrison towards the Boston & Maine railroad passenger station to the land of said railroad, and raise and appropriate money for the same.

12. To see if the town will vote to build a state road, so called, from the tracks of the Boston & Maine railroad near the freight depot at Ashland, beginning on the westerly side of said tracks by the residence of Frank Harris; Ross P. Sanborn to the New Hampton town line, and raise and appropriate money for the same.

13. To see if the town will vote to accept state aid for construction of new highways and repair of the state highways.

14. To see if the town will vote to establish a non-partisan electric light commission.

15. To see if the town will vote to ratify its vote taken at the biennial election November 7, 1916, rela-

tive to the expediency of acquiring or establishing an electric light plant and pass any vote relating thereto.

16. To see if the town will vote to purchase a town flag, and raise and appropriate money for the same.

17. To see what sum the town will vote as salary for Municipal Court Justice for the ensuing year.

18. To see if the town will vote to extend the town water on West Main street to Green Grove cemetery.

Given under our hands and seal, this seventeenth day of February, in the year of our Lord nineteen hundred and seventeen.

JOHN S. HUCKINS,
SELDON J. COTTON,
ALESSANDRO MORTON,

Selectmen of Ashland.

TOWN OFFICERS.

1916.

Town Clerk—Curt E.. Eastman.

Selectmen—John C. Huckins, Seldon J. Cotton, Alessandro Morton.

Treasurer—Ora A. Brown.

Tax Collector—Alba H. Carpenter.

Overseer of the Poor—Adolph G. Schelzel.

Janitor of Town Hall—Charles H. Heath.

Police—Ray C. Harriman.

Liquor Prosecuting Agent—Dona Guyotte.

Fire Wards—Lester G. Fifield, George F. Plummer, John B. Sullivan.

Superintendent of Water Works—Edgar W. Sanborn.

Superintendent of Fire Alarm—Lester G. Fifield.

Auditors—Edward P. Warner, Clifford E. Gingrass, John G. Smith.

Library Trustees—Lula B. Shepard, F. Anna Whipple, William F. Timlin.

INVENTORY.

Valuation of Town, April 1, 1916.

384 polls.		
190 horses,	$ 27,052	00
2 mules,	375	00
8 oxen,	875	00
154 cows,	8,327	00
18 neat stock,	1,017	00
67 sheep,	301	50
1 hog,	15	00
1,344 fowls,	1,037	50
101 vehicles and automobiles,	16,625	00
2 portable mills,	250	00
27 boats and launches,	5,520	00
Wood and lumber,	150	00
Stock in public funds,	19,241	00
Money on hand and at interest,	2,773	42
Stock in trade,	146,297	32
Mills and machinery,	305,987	50
Real estate,	790,974	00
Total valuation,	$1,326,818	23

Valuation by Districts.

District No. 1,	$1,162,333	23
District No. 2,	164,485	00
	$1,326,818	23

MONEY RAISED.

Town charegs,	$2,500	00
Town library.	250	00
Memorial day,	85	00
Highways and bridges,	3,300	00
Fire department,	650	00
Town poor,	100	00
Concrete streets and sidewalks,	500	00
Municipal court judge,	100	00
Town debt,	500	00
State tax,	2,137	50
County tax,	1,559	11
School money by law,	2,137	50
Extra school money, special district,	4,600	00
Notes and interest, special district,	1,960	00
Books and supplies, special district,	1,000	00
Repairs, special district,	500	00
Extra money, town district,	550	00
Overlay,	302	65
	$22,731	76

Town tax rate on $100.00	$1	00	
Special school district rate,		70	
			$1 70
Town tax rate on $100.00	$1	00	
Town school district rate,		34	
			$1 34

CURRENT EXPENSES.

MISCELLANEOUS BILLS.

The Record Print, printing town reports,	$ 60	00
W. J. Randolph, transfers,	2	30
U. S. Cons. Co., 1 blade,	7	00
C. E. Eastman, books,	3	51
Hughes & Gammons, insurance,	40	00
Studebaker Co., broom,	35	00
F. M. Harris, labor on inventory,	5	00
O. A. Brown, supplies,	1	50
Mary Murdock, labor,	1	25
J. G. Smith, on closets, selectmen's room,	19	35
James H. Mendell, on appraisal,	55	10
Ashland Electric Light Co., lights,	345	00
F. M. Harris, labor on inventory,	5	00
Penn Metal Co., culverts,	32	34
Good Roads Machine Co.,	1	50
Three men enlisted, car fare,	3	45
George I. Brown, bill,	5	38
John C. Huckins, bill, cash paid out,	12	82
North East Metal Culvert Co.,	82	20
S. J. Cotton, labor on dump,	9	00
Traffic Sign Co.,	5	25
C. H. Palmer, signs,		75
Ashland Electric Light Co., lights,	345	50
C. V. Knowlton, team for selectmen,	10	75
W. F. Timlin, expense on bank wall,	91	00
W. F. Timlin, expense on bank wall,	28	63
James Clifford, use of derrick,	8	00
North East Culvert Co.,	17	07
Edson C. Eastman, supplies,	1	28
W. F. Timlin, expense on bank wall,	50	60

Rumford Press, warrants,	18	50
Ashland Electric Light Co., lights,	347	00
R. M. Whitcomb & Co., supplies,	18	90
G. Conral Brummer, federal tax,	6	88
F. H. Chick, blacksmith bill,	3	05
J. Gardner Smith, labor on booths,	7	50
George I. Brown, miscellaneous bill,	7	75
Ashland Electric Light Co., lights,	347	50
Carey Furniture Co., supplies,	17	75
E. W. Sanborn, coal, hose house,	72	76
Asa Warren Drew, counsel,	25	00
Sullivan Bros., oil,		84
O. A. Brown, supplies,	8	75
O. A. Brown, supplies,	25	60
C. E. Eastman, supplies,	10	85
C. E. Eastman, copy inventory,	5	00
J. C. Huckins, cash paid out,	5	83
E. W. Sanborn, supplies,	2	05
	$2,217	04

BOARD OF HEALTH.

J. C. Huckins, vaccinating 113 children,	$113	00
A. E. Porter & Son, supplies,	11	85
A. Perley Fitch, supplies,	13	50
J. C. Huckins, vaccinating 30 children,	30	00
E. P. Warner, salary and supplies,	28	41
A. E. Porter & Son, supplies,	1	00
	$197	76

MEMORIAL DAY.

Appropriation,	$85	00
Paid F. M. Hughes, for G. A. R.,	$85	00

TOWN LIBRARY.

Appropriation,	$250 00
Paid Lula B. Shepard, trustee,	$250 00

TOWN POOR.

Eleanor Clifford, board of Moore child,	$ 42 00
Susie Deane, rent for F. Garland,	91 00
L. M. Orton, attendance on F. Garland,	10 25
	$143 25
Appropriation,	$100 00
Appropriation exceeded,	$43 25

FIRE DEPARTMENT.

W. B. Clifford, labor,	$ 4 30
Eureka Hose Mfg. Co., hose,	120 00
B. & M. R. R. fire,	16 41
B. & M. R. R. fire,	13 60
George F. Plummer, labor,	1 50
Pay roll, Hose Co. No. 1,	98 75
Pay roll, Hose Co. No. 2,	85 50
Pay roll, Hook & Ladder Co.,	65 50
Standard Extinguisher Co., supplies,	75 75
C. H. Palmer, janitor 1 year,	60 00
L. G. Fifield, salary and supplies,	54 83
O. A. Brown, supplies,	25 46
	$621 60

FIRE ALARM.

L. G. Fifield, services and supplies,	$180 76
Appropriation, fire department,	$650 00
Cash from B. & M. R. R.,	30 01

Cash from town of New Hampton,   16 40
                                                    _____
                                                    $696 41

Expended, fire department and on fire
                alarm system, $802 36

POLICE AND LOBBY EXPENSES.

C. E. Eastman, to May 1, 1917,   ` $ 11 25
J. H. Fleming, to May 1, 1917,   11 75
R. C. Harriman, salary,   514 09
C. H. Palmer, special,   10 00
J. G. Smith, special,   10 00
Fred A. Carr, special,   10 00   .
James H. Fleming, special,   10 00
Charles B. Marsh, labor,   75
                                            _____
                                            $577 84

TOWN OFFICERS' SALARIES.

Asa W. Drew, moderator, $ 9 00
C. H. Heath, supervisor, ballot clerk, and
                work on booths,   29 00
Fred A. Carr, ballot clerk,   9 00
C. V. Knowlton, supervisor,   26 00
W. F. Hardy, supervisor,   26 00
A. G. Schelzel, overseer of poor,   50 00
J. G. Smith, auditor and ballot clerk,   7 00
John E. Morrison, care of town clock,   25 00
E. P. Warner, auditor,   1 50
C. N. Swayne, ballot clerk,   3 00
Edna C. Goddard, librarian,   75 00
O. A. Brown, treasurer,   50 00
W. F. Timlin, ballot clerk,   6 00
C. E. Eastman, town clerk,   50 00

Seldon J. Cotton, selectman,	100	00
Alessandro Morton, selectman,	50	00
J. C. Huckins, selectman,	200	00
A. H. Carpenter, collector,	250	00
	$966	50

COST OF EDUCATION.

Special School District.

Receipts.

School money by law,	$1,872	45
Extra school money,	4,600	00
Books and supplies,	1,000	00
Repairs and renewals,	500	00
Notes and interest,	1,960	00
Proportion dog license,	107	22
Proportion literary fund,	180	73
Proportion state fund,	915	42
	$11,135	82

Expenditures.

Paid O. A. Brown, treasurer,	$11,135	8?

Ashland Town School District.

Receipts.

School money by law,	$265	05
Extra school money,	550	00
Proportion dog license,	15	18
Proportion literary fund,	25	58

Proportion state fund,	129	58

	$985	39

Paid Benjamin F. Pease, treasurer,	$985	39

POLICE COURT.

Asa W. Drew, Judge, salary 8 months,	$66	66

BOUNTIES PAID.

Orville Small, 7 hedgehogs,	$1	40
Elbridge Boynton, 1 hedgehog,		20
Howard Pease, 8 hedgehogs,	1	60
Charles Flanders, 1 hedgehog,		20
Floyd E. Huckins, 1 hedgehog,		20
Harold Taylor, 1 hedgehog,		20
George F. Plummer, 1 hedgehog,		20

	$4	00

SUMMARY OF HIGHWAY ACCOUNT.

Appropriation,	$3,300	00
Balance from 1915, state road fund,	62	00
Total available,	$3,362	00
Expended on state road,	$2,586	16
Received from state, $1,358 88		
Received from town Bridgewater, 49 87		
	$1,408	75
Cost to town,	$1,177	41
Balance on hand, town fund,	$45	29
Total expense state road,	$1,177	41

Total expense other highways,		2,309 77
Total expended,		$3,487 18
Exceeded appropriation,		$187 18

See report of road agents for details of expenditures.

RECAPITULATION.

Receipts.

Cash on hand Feb. 15, 1916,	$2,801 51
From tax collector,	22,181 05
From water rents,	2,582 03
From dog licenses,	112 80
Excise commission licenses,	6 16
Municipal court justice fines,	100 46
Pool tables and bowling alleys,	66 25
Moving picture and show licenses,	253 00
Peddlers' licenses,	8 00
B. & M. R. R . fire account,	30 01
Town of New Hampton, fire account,	16 40
Town of Bridgewater, highway account,	49 87
Town of Center Harbor, use of roll,	10 00
Refund on material bought,	1 00
Old stove sold,	2 00
Janitor town hall,	60
Rent town shed,	10 00
Rent old Masonic hall,	24 50
Junk dealers' licenses,	24 00
State treasurer, bounties paid,	3 20
State treasurer, highway account,	1,358 88
State treasurer, insurance tax,	22 50
State treasurer, railroad tax,	225 17
State treasurer, savings bank tax,	2,017 61
State treasurer, literary fund,	206 31
State treasurer, school fund,	1,045 00
Town notes,	2,000 00

$35,158.31

Expenditures.

Miscellaneous bills,	$2,217 04
State tax,	2,137 50
County tax,	1,559 11
·Fire department,	621 60
Fire alarm,	180 76
Board of health,	197 76
Memorial day,	85 00
State road,	2,586 16
Other highways,	2,309 77
Town library,	250 00
Town poor,	143 25
Police and lobby,	577 84
Police court,	66 66
Bounties paid,	4 00
County poor,	12 77
Town officers,	966 50
Schools, special· district,	11,135 82
Schools, town district,	985 39
Notes and interest,	5,929 18
Cash on hand,	3,192 20
	$35,158 31

Report of the Trust Funds, Feb. 15, 1917.

Date	Trust Funds—Purpose of Creation	How Invested	Am't of Principal	Rate of Int'st
19.6				
July 8	Martha Cummings. For the care and preservation of family lot in Green Grove Cemetery in Ashland N. H.	Ashland Savings Bank	$200.00	3 1-2
1917				
Jan 27	Horace W. Berry, For highway purposes	Ashland Savings Bank	$1,411.13	3 1-2

FINANCIAL STATEMENT.

Feb. 15, 1917.

Receipts.

Cash on hand Feb. 15, 1916,	$2,801 51
Receipts during the year,	32,356 80
	$35,158 31

Disbursements.

Disbursements during year,	$31,966 11
Cash on hand Feb. 15, 1917,	3,192 20
	$35,158 31

Assets.

Cash on hand Feb. 15, 1917,	$3,192 20
Due from state, hedgehog bounty,	2 00
	$3,194 20

Liabilities.

Due on shade tree appropriation,	$ 48 55
Due on state road fund,	45 29
Due on town notes,	30,382 20
	$30,476 04
Balance against town Feb. 15, 1916,	$30,493 07
Balance against town Feb. 15, 1917,	$27,281 84
Decrease of town debt during year,	$3,211 23

TREASURER'S REPORT.

Receipts.

Cash on hand from last year,	$2,801	51
From tax collector,	22,181	05
Superintendent of water works,		
water rents,	2,582	03
Town clerk, dog licenses,	112	80
Excise commission, license account,	6	16
Ashland Savings Bank, note,	2,000	00
State treasurer,	3,516	59
Asa W. Drew, municipal court account,	100	46
Selectmen on sundry accounts,	1,857	71
	$35,158	31

Disbursements..

Paid Selectmen's orders,	$23,899	43
State tax,	2,137	50
Ashland Savings Bank, note,	2,016	67
Eunice A. Peaslee, on note,	182	98
Sarah E. Chamberlin, on note,	142	10
Martha A Heath, on note,	70	00
Mary J. Horrigan, on note,	24	50
Daniel C. Hill, on note,	50	75
Mabell N. Campbell, on note,	10	50
Henry C. Dearborn, on note,	10	50
Elizabeth A. Hodgson, on note,	56	00
Jessie A. Thompson, on note,	35	00
Wm. Bateman, on notes,	43	75
Francella C. Perkins, on note,	2,694	93
F. P. Nichols, on note,	56	00
Minnie L. Smith, on note,	84	00

Henry M. Smith, on note,	196	00
M. C. Blake, on note,	87	50
George W. Andrews, on note,	28	00
Margaret J. Gordon, on note,	14	00
Emma H. Scribner, on note,	52	50
Sarah A. Boynton, on note,	52	50
Nellie E. Plummer, on note,	21	00
Cash on hand,	3,192	20
	$35,158	31

We hereby certify that we have carefully examined the foregoing accounts of O. A. Brown, Town Treasurer, and find them correctly cast and properly vouched.

C. E. GINGRAS,
J. G. SMITH,
Auditors.

February 26, 1917.

REPORT OF HIGHWAY AGENT.

John H. Blanchard, agent,	$102 32
S. J. Cotton,	13 50
Frank Moore,	11 90
Charles Clough,	1 68
E. W. Sanborn,	8 50
Ray Harriman,	6 00
Benjamin Dean,	133 75
Henry Dion,	13 00
W. B. Clifford,	12 00
George McKinley,	5 54
H. E. Heath,	1 32
William Ryan,	4 00
M. Landrock,	4 55
Henry Dion,	7 00
W. B. Clifford,	1 32
George McKinley,	5 32
William Ryan,	4 00
M. Landrock,	2 00
Benjamin Dean,	18 62
W. F. Timlin, agent,	12 90
W. F. Timlin, agent,	15 00
Henry Dion,	4 22
Bolts for street sweeper,	35
E. Archer,	40
B. & M. R. R.,31 loads gravel at 15c, (1915),	4 65
Frank Moore,	102 50
Squam Lake Lumber Co.,	4 32
Geo. W. Plummer & Son,	85
Allen Howe,	5 20
St. Arnold,	3 35
Benjamin Dean,	132 25

W. F. Timlin, agent,	32	00
Frank Moore,	94	72
W. D. Philbrick,	2	25
Willis Clark,	2	64
J. Brown,		90
E. W. Boynton,	10	00
American Express Co.,		30
C. V. Knowlton,		50
O. A. Brown,	14	54
F. H. Chick,	18	57
Benjamin Dean,	120	97
W. F. Timlin, agent,	48	00
Benjamin Dean,	58	70
E. G. Boynton,	2	00
Joseph Benton,	3	50
George Lambert,	21	00
Benjamin Dean,	15	50
W. B. Smith, Dist.,	77	25
Squam Lake Lumber Co.,	2	40
J. G. Smith,	1	50
J. O. Clark,	9	25
A. F. Nichols,	20	00
Benjamin Dean,	170	79
W. F. Timlin, agent,	27	00
F. D. Eastman,	3	50
Benjamin Dean,	15	50
W. F. Timlin, agent,	3	00
Benjamin Dean,	6	50
W. F. Timlin, agent,	3	00
Benjamin Dean,	96	47
J. O. Clark,	5	00
W. F. Timlin, agent,	15	50
Rufus Blake,	2	00
W. L. Brown,	7	00
Benjamin Dean,	81	65

Henry Gault,	9	75
J. O. Clark,	7	12
W. F. Timlin, agent,	42	60
Freight,		53
Walter B. Brown,	4	56
Benjamin Dean,	65	50
J. O. Clark,	5	62
W. F. Timlin, agent,	17	00
Frank Moore,	13	25
Benjamin Dean,	.2	25
Squam Lake Lumber Co.,	3	29
Benjamin Dean,	43	12
George Bryant, 75 loads gravel,	7	50
S. J. Cotton, 41 loads gravel,	6	15
Allen Howe, 27 loads gravel,	4	05
Mrs. Curtis, 12 loads gravel,	2	40
Frederick M. Merrow, 10 loads gravel,	1	50
Benjamin Dean,	30	00
Frank Moore,	21	80
George Lambert,	6	00
F. D. Eastman,	22	50
W. F. Timlin, agent,	13	00
G. B. Peavey,	3	45
O. A. Brown,	35	26
A. F. Nichols,	20	50
E. W. Sanborn,	70	69
Hollis Heath,	2	00
Benjamin Dean,	124	00
C. H. Sanborn,	17	80
Town of Holderness,	6	00
F. D. Eastman,	32	50
Frank Moore,	16	12
W. B. Smith,	16	25

$ 2,309 77

W. F. TIMLIN, Highway Agent.

TRUNK LINE MAINTENANCE.

O. L. Stevens, with team,	$633 25
S. J. Cotton, teams,	256 86
S. J. Cotton, patrolman,	85 00
Ed Bennett,	31 00
George Sorrell,	45 50
Frank Lougee,	76 11
Frank Sorrell,	100 00
George McKinley,	24 50
John Hutton,	22 50
Will Clark,	6 00
Clarence Robinson,	1 31
Enoch Archer,	30 00
Robert Dean,	107 03
John Comier,	18 50
John Blanchard,	2 00
Allen Howe, gravel,	84 85
Squam Lake Lumber Co.,	53 48
F. H. Chick, blacksmith,	40
Herman Lougee,	58 00
Walter Preston,	42 00
Charles Paris,	45 00
Jed Brown,	9 00
Alex Ricker,	6 00
Patrolman's dinner,	75
Ed W. Sanborn,	3 90
Mrs. Curtis,	49 15
	$1,792 09

S. J. COTTON, Patrolman.

REPORT OF NEW TARVIA ROAD.

S. J. Cotton, Agent,	$ 70 00
S. J. Cotton, teams,	140 00
S. J. Cotton,	140 00
Ed'Bennett,	38 00
George Sorrell,	16 00
Frank Lougee,	38 48
George McKinley,	51 00
Will Clark,	36 00
Freight, express and demurrage on stone,	211 12
Telephone,	81
Otto Willoughby,	9 00
Henry Vachon,	51 55
Enoch Archer,	6 00
Al. Brown,	8 75
Fred Normandy,	41 11
Jim Clark,	7 00
Clarence Robinson,	19 25
Frank St. Arnold,	2 00
Joe Fields,	2 00
Frank Sorrell,	22 00
Tom Billodeau,	6 00
Joe Billodeau,	6 00
L. W. Packard, coal,	12 00
	$794 07

S. J. COTTON. Patrolman.

SETTLEMENT WITH TAX COLLECTOR.

Receipts.

Taxes as per warrant,	$22,731 76
Added by collector,	32 00
Interest,	27 80
	$22,791 56

Expenditures.

Treasurer's receipts,	$22,181 05
Discounts allowed,	561 96
Abatements,	84 55
	$22,791 56

JANITOR'S REPORT.

Feb. 15, 1917.

Receipts.

1916

Feb.	17, Tinker's Orchestra,	$ 6 00
	23, Entertainment Club,	4 00
Mar.	21, Entertainment Club,	3 75
Apr.	24, High school,	3 00
	27, Pythian Sisters,	4 00
	30, St. Mark's church,	3 00
May	5, St. Mark's church,	14 00
	12, Hose Company,	4 00
June	14, Kentucky Girl,	6 00
	19, Empire Company,	6 00
Aug.	4, St. Agnes' church,	4 00
	10, Episcopal church,	6 00
Sept.	15, Cow Boy,	5 00
Oct.	13, Baptist church,	10 00
Dec.	27, Tinker's Orchestra,	6 00

1917.

Jan.	3, Basket ball,	3 00
	27, Basket ball,	3 00
Feb.	1, Basket ball,	3 50
	9, Basket ball,	4 00
	13, Grammar school,	3 50
	15, Methodist church,	10 00

$111 75

Expenditures.

Electric lights,	$12 60
1 yale lock,	1 75
2 door pulls,	15
1 can dustbane,	2 75
3 dozen hooks,	1 50
Sawing wood,	1 08
Cleaning hall,	1 50
Leon Page,	50
Sawdust,	1 00
Yale lock,	2 00
Cleaning hall yard,	3 00
Putting on lock,	75
Ed Sanborn, stair rails,	5 00
Helping Ed Sanborn,	2 00
Frank Estes, water bubbler,	6 60
Dustbane,	48
Cleaning hall,	1 50
1 cord slab wood,	2 50
1 cord hard wood,	5 00
Sawing wood,	1 50
A, E. Porter, use of piano,	9 00
Kerosene oil and meal,	49
Care of hall,	48 50
Paid town,	60

$111 75

C. H. HEATH, Janitor.

ASHLAND TOWN LIBRARY.

Treasurer's Report for Year Ending Feb. 15, 1917.

Dr.

Cash received from town treasurer, for support of library,	$250	00
Cash on hand,	52	83
Cash received from librarian for fines, cards, etc.,	4	72
	$307	55

Cr.

Hughes & Gammons, premium on policy,	$31	25
A. F. Whipple, books,	3	15
F. L. Barnard & Co., book binders,	32	51
Set of Shakespeare's Works,	10	00
A. E. Porter & Son, books,	156	61
Gaylord Bros,. supplies,	23	64
Library Bureau, supplies,	20	85
Changing cabinet,	1	55
Changing cards,	2	00
Duster,		50
Freight,		79
Express,		52
Cash unexpended,	24	18
	$307	55

Balance on hand Feb. 15, 1917, $24 18

LULA B. SHEPARD, Treasurer.

REPORT OF LIBRARY TRUSTEES.

To the Citizens of Ashland:

We respectfully submit the fourth annual report of the Library Trustees. During the year 7,526 books were taken out, of which number 216 were non-fiction. 54 books, all of more than common value, were given during the year. The number of books added was 158. We have a complete record of 3,200 books and estimate those not yet listed to be 400. With nearly four thousand volumes it must be apparent to all that we are fast out-growing our limited quarters in the Town Building and should begin to make plans for accommodations more up-to-date and in keeping with our needs. It might be said in this connection that we should have a reading room containing daily papers and magazines and open to the public, evenings.

F. ANNA WHIPPLE,
LULA B. SHEPARD,
W. F. TIMLIN,

Library Trustees.

REPORT OF FIRE WARDS.

To the Citizens of Ashland, we respectfully submit the annual report of the Fire Wards:

April 17, 2-2-2 rung for fire which destroyed the dwelling home of George Parkhurst in New Hampton.

May 3, alarm from box 45 for fire in building owned by Hazen Baker and occupied by Ed Sweeney. Chemicals used. Damage of $3.00 was paid by insurance company.

May 11, 2-2-2, brush fire back of mills and cemetery.

May 13, still alarm; brush fire on land of B. & M. R. R.

June 21, still alarm for fire which destroyed the barn owned by Helen McMillan.

Nov. 13, alarm from box 41 for fire in building owned by Mrs. A. F. Nichols and occupied by Moran & Fifield. Chemicals used. Building insured for $800. Insurance of $30 paid. Contents insured for $2,000. Damage of $75 paid.

Dec. 15, alarm from box 59, for fire in B. & M. freight car at station. Loss $500.00.

Dec. 25, alarm from box 66 for chimney fire at Fred Guyotte's.

Jan. 8, 1917, still alarm for chimney fire at Joe Zeberg's.

Feb. 6, still alarm for chimney fire at E. A. Straw's.

Feb. 10, alarm from box 62, for chimney fire in house owned by Mrs. S. E. Ellis. Chemicals used. No loss.

Dec. 25, still alarm for chimney fire at Herbert Brown's.

Our equipment is in good shape and we need nothing new at the present time.

In the death of Fireward John B. Sullivan, which occurred on Jan. 12, the members of the Ashland Fire Department feel they sustained the loss of a capable and efficient officer, whose interest in the department was shown on many occasions, and his loss is greatly regretted by all.

L. G. FIFIELD,

GEORGE F. PLUMMER,

Fire Wards.

REPORT OF CHIEF OF POLICE.

From May 1, 1916, to Feb. 15, 1917.

Number of arrests made and held for court, as follows:

For peddling fruit without a license,	1
For drunkenness,	4
Automobile speeding,	1
Automobiles without number plates,	1
Motor cycle speeding,	2
For larceny,	1
For selling Uno beer,	1
For assault,	1
Total number of arrests,	12
Held for out of town officers,	3
Locked up for safe keeping,	3
Number of business places found open,	1
Number put up for lodging,	101

Respectfully reported,

R. C. HARRIMAN, Chief of Police.

REPORT OF MUNICIPAL COURT.

This court was established the latter part of May, 1916, and was ready for business June 1, 1916, since which there have been 21 cases brought to the attention of the court, 20 on the criminal docket and one on the civil docket.

The list of cases on the criminal docket are classified as follows

For peddling foreign fruits without a license,	1
Non-support of wife and children,	4
Assault and battery,	3
Overspeeding of motor vehicles,	4,
Non-display of number plate,	1
Larceny,	1
Bastardy,	1
Drunkenness,	4
Sale of spirituous liquors,	1

On the criminal list there have been collected in fines and costs as per report to town treasurer, $132 25

Accounted for as follows:

Paid special police officer, James H. Flemming,	$13 05	
Paid account of assistance and keeping prisoners,	2 75	
Paid witness fees,	2 74	
Paid for court seal, stationery and necessary supplies,	13 25	
		$31 79

Balance to town treasurer, $100 46

Respectfully submitted,

ASA WARREN DREW.

WATER WORKS REPORT.

Dr.

Received for water rent,	$2,989 51

Cr.

Paid New Hampton tax,	$ 46	20
W. B. Brown,		75
Walter Preston,	13	00
Sherman Clark,	2	50
Tom Coleman,	1	25
The Hawthorne Press,	7	50
O. A. Brown,	2	43
E. W. Sanborn, for stock, supplies and labor for new services tapped and old services renewed, and other incidental expenses connected with the water works,	208	55
Salary of superintendent,	125	00
For index books,		30
O. A. Brown, treasurer,	2,582	03
	$2,989	51

Respectfully submitted,

E. W. SANBORN, Superintendent.

AUDITOR'S REPORT.

The undersigned have examined the foregoing accounts of the Town of Ashland and find them correctly cast and properly vouched.

CLIFFORD E. GINGRAS,
J. G. SMITH,

Auditors.

Feb. 26, 1917.

Births Registered in the Town of Ashland, N. H., ... e Year Ending Decem ..

Name of Child (If any)	Male or Female	Living or Stillborn	No. child 1st, 2d &c	Color	Name of Father	Maiden Name of Mother	Color of Parents	Residence of Parents	Occupation of Father	Birthplace of Father	Birthplace of Mother
ard T	M	Liv'g	2	W	John B May	...il Worcester	W	Newton Mass	Physician	Newton Mass	Newton Mass
yn M	F	"	1	"	Harry A Smith	...sa M Dupuis	"	Ashd	Telg'h oper	Plymouth	Pittsfield
red Alberta	M	"	8	"	...nk G ...mod	Alice M ...ine	"	Ashd	Laborer	Campton	Bridgewater
uel Herbert	F	"	2	"	...us C Eastman	Elsie L Spiller	"	Ashland	Carpenter	Holderness	Bridgewater
	M	"	2	"	Horace S Plummer	Eva A Sawyer	"	Ashd	Sawyer	Thornton	Campton
ley Alfred	F	"	3	"	Horace S Plummer	Eva A Sawyer	"	Ashd	Sawyer	Thornton	...ton
n ...ay	M	"	3	"	Thos A B land	Iva P Williams	"	Ashland	Teamster	P E Island	Lyman
es Herman	F	"	8	"	L ... C Hammond	...nie H ...her	"	Ashd	Farmer	Northfield Vt	Sherbr'ke P
vina	F	"	2	"	W M Downer	Edith Blanchard	"	Ashd	Laborer	Groveton	Ashland
es Franklin	M	"	3	"	Emile ...te	Alice Merchant	"	Ashd	Laborer	Canada	...la
Shepard	F	"	1	"	Harry Bantt	Edith ...nes	"	Bridgewater	Fruit dealer	Bridgewater	La onia
d Wilson	M	"	4	"	Raffaello Puccetti	Assunta Caser	"	Ashland	...lk	...laly	Italy
old R	F	"	3	"	...ldt E Burt	Edna Wilson	"	Ashland	...lk	Sutton P Q	Harcourt N
ence M	F	"	3	"	Roy A Wilkins	Floren o ...rmette	"	Ashland	Laborer	Kirby Vt	Franconia
ren S	M	"	1	"	Th ... ...l mon	Lucy Guyotte	"	Ashland	Painter	...va Scotia	Ashland
l Clifford	"	"	1	"	Warr ... Downing	...e Fellows	"	Ashland	Laborer	Center Harbor	Ireland
	"	"	2	"	Charles Ashley	Ada Jacobs	"	Ashland	Laborer	England	Lebanon
othy Belle	"	"	2	"	Henry Provencial	Leona E Ruel	"	Ashland	Laborer	Canada	Littleton
y Beatrice	F	S B	5	"	Henry Provencial	L ...va E Ruel	"	Ashland	Real est d'l'r	Canada	...ton
ard Rixford	M	Liv'g	1	"	John Harri ...on	Selina M Gerourard	"	Ashland	Laborer	Bethlehem	Canada
old D nadd	"	"	3	"	Alfred H Bogean	Antounette Gamache	"	Ashd	Farmer	St Albans Vt	Ashland
	M	"	2	"	Abner F Jackson	Carrie M Fowler	"	Ashland	Laborer	Ashland	Newbury
ginia Ruth	"	"	3	"	Joseph ... Brown	Alma Duchane	"	Ashd	Laborer	...la	Canada
nd Clark	F	S B	10	"	Albert L Brown	Mary L Martell	"	Ashland	...rer	Ashland	N Bedford M
old Loue	M	Liv'g	4	"	Albert L Brown	Mary L ...ll	"	Ashland	Chauffeur	Ashland	N Bedford M
er Earl	"	"	1	"	Almon E Carter	Addie L Webster	"	...and	Barber	Sandwich	Sandwich
n Martha	F	"	5	"	Arthur Harriman	Annie Landry	"	Ashd	...lk	Ashland	Providence R
il ...ita	M	"	1	"	Percy R Lewis	Ruth C Brown	"	Ashland	Farmer	N Bedford M...s	Ashland
	"	"	1	"	Orin Amsden	Elsie Clark	"	Ashland	Printer	Meredith	N Hampton
	"	"	2	"	Loue Day	Theresa ...te	"	Ashland	Chauffeur	Haverhill	Holderness
	"	"	8	"	Ernest ...le	Pauline I Stanley	"	Ashland	Fireman	Whitefield	Epsom
	F	"	1	"	John O'Shea	Martha Moulton	"	Ashland	Soldier U S A	Plymouth	Belmont
	"	"		"	J ...hn J Hurley	Lily F Kelley	"	Ashland		Ireland	Highgate Vt

Place Marriage	Name and Surname of Groom and Bride	Residence of each at time of Marriage		Occupation of Groom and Bride	Place of Birth of each	Name of Parents	Birthplace of Parents	Occupation of Parents		Name, and ...
ymouth	Max Weisberg	ꞏꞏꞏꞏ	31 W	Machine t'd'r	Warsaw Rus	ꞏꞏꞏ Weisberg	Germany	Mill hd	2	Rev A
ymouth	Flora B Vallier	Ashland	33 "	Mill hand	ꞏꞏꞏ	Genette Weisb'rg	Nw Hampshire	Mill l nd	2	Rev A
ꞏꞏꞏ	Norman Parsons	Ashl nd	28 "	Laborer	Newfoundll'd	Arthur A Clark	Newfoundland	ꞏꞏꞏter	1	
shland	Cora Marston	Ashland	31 "	Nurse	Ctr Harbor	ꞏꞏ H Long				
						J hn Parsons				
						Polly Marston				
ashland	ꞏꞏ Wd	Boston Mss	31 "	ꞏo finisher	London Eng	Go H Hawkins	Ctr Harbor	Farmer	2	Fr P J
	Barbara A	Boston Mss	19 "	ꞏꞏt	ꞏꞏla	Mary Plaisted	London Eng	ꞏꞏr	1	
	Burgoyne					John Wd	London Eng			
						Rose Lazaras				
anches'r	Bon A Coley	Ashland	22 "	Clerk	Ashland	ꞏꞏs Burgoyne	Ga	Farmer	1	Rev M
						Anna Stars	Tamworth			
						Almon W Cooley				
	Bessie M Towle	Manchester	22 "	Stenogra'r	Manchester	My A Horner	ꞏꞏlock Vt	Super't	1	
						Henry W ꞏꞏe	Hampton			
aconia	Richard Cox	Ashland	45 "	Fireman	ꞏꞏd	Bula A Nason	Candia	Laborer	1	Rev. E
						John Cox	England			
aconia	Mary L Chase	Ashland	49 "	ꞏꞏr	Rumney	ꞏ ꞏn Rackham	Ga	Laborer	3	
						ꞏꞏe Sorrell				
aconia	Grover E Patten	Laconia	20 "	ꞏꞏst	ꞏꞏa	Flora ꞏꞏtte	Alexandria	Farmer	1	Rev
						Go Patten	Alexandria			
	ꞏꞏe E	Ashland	23 "	Mill operat'e	ꞏꞏd	Phylona Patten	Concord	Brakeman	ꞏ	
	Whitcher					Burt ꞏꞏr	Bristol			
shland	Gus W Pattee	Ashland	26 "	Merchant	Wilmot	Cora Hazelton	Wilmot	ꞏꞏt	1	Rev J
						Gus H ꞏꞏe	Williston Vt			
	Agnes D Burke	Pl ꞏꞏgh	22 "	ꞏ	Williston Vt	Susie W Morey	Richmond	Blacksmith	1	
						Gordon Burke				
						ꞏꞏe Keefe				

Cause of Death	Maiden Name of Mother	Name of Father	Place of Birth (Father)	Place of Birth (Mother)	Occupation	Single, mar. or widowed	Color	Male or Female	Place of Birth	Years	Months	Days
Pneumonia	Jennie Vallier	Lougie Bexror	Westbury Ct	Ashland		S	W	M	Ashland	80	2	14
Heart failure	Sally Thur'ton	John L Hodgdon	Northfield	Bridgewater	Stone mason	W	:	:	Northfield Me	68	5	11
Cer'l hemor'ge	Hannah Harding	Edward Avery			Clergyman	M	:	:	Prospect Me		6	35
Premature birth	Eva Sawyer	Horace Plummer	Thornton	r tón			:	F	Ashland			21
Premature birth	Eva Sawyer	Horace Plummer	Thornton	pón		S	:	M	Ashland		6	
Pneumonia	Sarah C Fowle	Joseph McGraw	N B	Wel'g'f'd Ct	Student	:	:	F	Ashland	14	4	20
Epitheloma	Go W Fowle	Geo W Shepard	Holderness	Holderness	Retired	M	:	M	Holderness	63		
Asphyxiated	Jessie M Hardy	George Mack		Rumney			:		Ashland		9	13
Arteroschrosis	My Avery	Jonathan Dustin	Thornton		Housewife	M	:	F	Westville N Y	74	9	25
Pneumonia	Ol'e Orousard	Frank	Canada	Ca ada		S	:	M	Ashl'd	1		
Int'l nephritis	Ella	Daniel Bowen	Ireland	Ireland		W	:	F	Boston Mass	60		28
Pneumonia	Minnie Ruel	Henry Provenc'r	P Q				:	M	Ashland			
Stil born	Laura Gamache	Fred Brazeau	St Albans Vt			S	:	:	Ashland	20	5	15
Pul'y tuberculo's	Julia Lamond	Eugene	Canada	Ashland	House work		:	:	Ashl'nd	88	8	11
Stillborn	Mary Gte	John A Perkins	Holderness	Canada	Nurse	S	:	F	Holderness	52		13
Cer'l apoplexy	Caroline Thyran	bcR Baker	Holderness	Goveton		:	:	:	Thornton		1	16
Pellagra	Anne Landry	Abel Wallace	Sandwich	Meredith		W	:	M	Windham	78	11	7
Stillborn	Martha Clark	Arthur Hart'man	Ashland	S ndwich	Retired	M	:	F	Cedar L'k N S	55	7	22
er'? anemia	Louise Kelley	Barnet Hughes		Provd'ce R I	Motorman	:	:	M	Holderness	56	7	18
Appendicitis	Arrer Hall	Wm Shields	N S	Franklin	Housewife	:	:	:	Ashland	52	3	22
Per's anemia	Maria Hackett	Jos E Reeves	Andover	Ieland		S	:	F	Ashland	21	1	16
Tuberculosis	Sarah J Andrews	Frank'n Scribner	Littleton	N S	Clerk	W	:	M	N Hampton	75	5	20
Apoplexy	Ruth B Sargent	Chas L Gordon	Sanbornton	N Hampton		M	:	F	Maine	65	6	12
Illis colitis	Mary L Martell	John Rollins	Ashland	Holderness	Housewife	:	:	:	Holderness	47	2	1
...t disease	Hannah Annis	Albert L Bown		Plymouth	Housewife	:	:	:	Holderness	57	4	9
Per's anemia	Sarah H Lowd	Cushing	Maine	Canada	Housewife	:	:	:	Farmington	58	2	16
Carcem'a of h.i's	Mary Blanchard	John B	Holderness	Maine	Shoemaker	:	:	M	Bridgewater	57		23
Arteriochrosis	Betsy Farn wo'h	Geo Shepard	Holderness	Holderness	Hotel Prop'r	W	:	F	Bridgewater	65	9	1
Arteriorschrosis	Mary J Plummer	Gus Adams		Holderness	Retired	W	:	:	N Hampton	70	3	3
Complications		Dan'l Batchelder	Bridgewater		Retired		:	M	Holderness			
Cer'b'l hemor'ge	Eth Lock	Frank O Kelley	Bridgewater	Meredith			:	:	Holderness	83	9	26
Stillborn	Anna Morrison	Person Cheney	Jay Vt	Wat'v'le Vt		S	:	M		76	3	20
Pneumonia		Zebulon Sinclair	N Hampton	Sanbornton								
Septicemea			Moultonb'o									

C. E. EASTMAN, Town Clerk.

SCHOOL REPORT

ASHLAND SPECIAL SCHOOL DISTRICT.

Report of the Treasurer of the School Board for Year Ending

February 15, 1917.

Receipts.

Balance on hand from last year,	$ 949 01
From Mrs. F. S. Edwards, for supplies,	1 40
F. W. Knight, telephone and supplies,	1 65
Ida Mann, tuning fork sold,	52
Ashland Town School District, tuition,	40 00
New Hampton School District, tuition,	214 64
Gilford School District, tuition,	26 67
Holderness School District, tuition,	98 88
Sandwich School District, tuition,	26 67
Zenas B. Furbush, tuition,	20 00
Frank O. Kelley, tuition,	9 00
Lewis Sherburne, tuition,	3 50
Almon Huckins, tuition,	15 00
Guy Torsey, tuition,	10 00
Town treasurer,	11,135 82
	$12,552 76

Expenditures.

Paid F. W. Knight, salary,	$1,355 54
Mary E. Smith, salary,	208 35
Marguerite Poore, salary,	249 98
Florence P. Hubbard, salary,	349 97
Emelyn G. Nickerson, salary,	320 78
Mary Roberts, salary.	432 00
Mildred E. Smith, salary,	432 00

Blanche Rogers, salary,	432 00
Minnie M. Thompson, salary,	432 00
Marjorie B. Boothe, salary,	165 00
Anna B. Carrigan, salary,	165 00
Lillian Carmichael, salary,	180 00
Mary S. Ireland, salary,	180 00
Cora P. Clay, salary,	240 00
Ida Mann, salary,	252 00
Anne Lawrence, salary,	252 00
Emily E. Cook, salary,	246 00
M. M. Morey, salary janitor,	504 00
M. M. Morey, extra labor,	70 50
M. M. Morey, truant officer,	25 00
L. G. Fifield, labor and supplies,	23 36
Ashland Electric Light Co., lights,	48 30
E. W. Sanborn, coal,	1,438 77
White Mt. Tel. & Tel. Co., telephone,	20 23
E. G. Boynton, wood,	63 00
Geo. E. Huckins, milk,	1 72
George W. Lambert, wood,	103 50
Houghton, Mifflin & Co., text books,	3 17
American Book Co., text books,	76 23
Ginn & Co., text books,	113 45
Silver, Burdett & Co., text books,	43 02
Benjamin H. Sanborn & Co., text books,	7 15
McKinley Publishing Co., text books,	5 03
D. C. Heath & Co., text books,	9 67
Allyn & Bacon, text books,	31 54
University of Chicago Press, text books,	1 14
Little, Brown & Co., text books,	14 71
A. Schelzel, supplies,	55
W. B. Brown, supplies,	4 90
Carr Brothers, supplies,	1 87
Beal & Hartwell, supplies,	1 96
Ashland Pharmacy, supplies,	55

L. W. Wilbur, equipment,	22 73
Carey Furniture Co., equipment,	15 65
Edward E. Babb & Co., supplies,	287 59
O. A. Brown, supplies,	166 10
W. F. Timlin, supplies,	40
The People's Market, supplies,	3 34
R. E. Lane, supplies,	1 79
Orient Spray Co., supplies,	58 05
Howard & Brown, supplies,	15 56
The Chemical Rubber Co., supplies,	12 00
C. C. Birchard Co., text books,	2 47
F. A. Kimball, sawing wood,	7 50
J. W. Boynton, sawing wood,	23 75
J. G. Smith, labor, sawing wood,	2 33
Frank G. Estes, sawing wood,	1 43
American Express Co.,	35
Robert A. Foss, services and supplies,	19 50
Alice Hughes, laundry work,	4 75
F. H. Osgood, musical instruction and expense,	122 71
Alice Knowlton, services,	1 00
Henry W. Wells, map,	2 50
C. H. Heath, services,	1 00
C. V. Knowlton, team,	1 00
Lewis E. Eastman, labor and material,	151 03
F. W. Knight, enumeration,	10 00
I. M. Brown, services,	4 20
F. C. Merrill, tuning piano,	2 50
E. W. Sanborn, labor and supplies,	52 72
C. H. Palmer, labor and supplies,	5 67
George I. Brown, labor and money paid out,	6 71
Frank Fifield, labor and supplies,	36 14
J. L. Hammett Co., supplies,	46 49
The Century Co., text books,	10 00
Alice E. Hilliard, teaching,	14 00

Theodore Jacques, supplies,	5	75
American Cookery, text books,	1	00
Stone & Underhill Co., supplies,		41
Herman Goldberger, magazines,	16	25
Cambridge Botanical Supply Co., supplies,	108	73
F. W. Knight, incidentals,	17	57
Cambridge Trust Co., note,	1,053	33
Blanche M. Nichols, note and interest,	617	50
Henry M. Smith, interest,	200	00
Hiram J. Merrill, interest,	24	00
Lucy A. Merrill, interest,	20	00
Francella C. Perkins, interest,	20	00
Marsena C. Blake, interest,	36	00
Frances Plummer, interest,	20	00
Balance on hand,	793	32
	$12,552	76

SUMMARY OF FINANCES.

Revenue—Current.

Balance from last year,	$ 949	01
Entire amount of money required by law to be raised for schools, 1916,	1,872	45
Entire additional amount voted at school meeting, 1916,	4,600	00
Amount assessed to pay for necessary school books and supplies,	1,000	00
Amount of literary fund received from state, December, 1916,	180	73
Amount received from state treasurer, under chapter 158 of the Sessions Laws of 1909, December, 1916,	915	42
Amount received from dog licenses, April, 1916,	107	22
Amount received from all other sources not included in above,	467	93
Total revenue for current expenses,	$10,092	76

Extraordinary.

Amount raised for repairs and remodeling, 1916,	$ 500	00
Amount raised to pay district debt,	1,500	00
Amount raised to pay interest,	460	00
Total extraordinary revenue,	$2,460	00

Expenditures—Current.

Amount expended for text books,	$324	29
Amount expended for reference books, maps, and other apparatus,	100	97

Amount expended for scholars supplies,	414	94
Amount expended for teachers' salaries, regular,	5,906	62
Amount expended for salaries of special activities,	122	71
Amount paid for truant officer, including enumeration of children,	35	00
Amount paid for minor repairs,	243	65
Amount paid for janitor,	504	00
Amount paid for building supplies,	224	56
Amount paid for fuel,	1,636	52
Amount paid for light,	48	30
Amount unclassified expenditures not included above,	162	37
Total current expenditures,	$9,723	93

Extraordinary.

Amount paid for replacement of equipment,	$44	68

Payments of Debt and Interest.

Amount paid on debt,	$1,500	00
Amount paid for interest on debt,	490	83
Total debt and interest payments,	$1,990	83
Grand total expenditures,	$11,759	44
Total outstanding district indebtedness,	$10,000	00

Respectfully submitted,

O. A. BROWN, Treasurer.

We hereby certify that we have carefully examined the foregoing accounts of O. A. Brown, treasurer, and find them correctly cast and properly vouched.

FRANK FIFIELD,
ALBERT E. PORTER,

Auditors, Special School District.

REPORT OF THE PUBLIC SCHOOLS.

ASHLAND SPECIAL SCHOOL DISTIRCT.

To the Citizens of Ashland:

The schools of the special district are, as during the past few years, under the supervision of the High school principal. In the grades and the High school the work of instruction has been uniformly satisfactory. Teachers, elected to fill vacancies caused by resignations of the preceding year, are fitting into their positions efficiently. The present registration of the schools shows a total of 239, 108 boys and 131 girls. This is a gain of 27 pupils according to the report for last year. Attendance has been remarkably good this year, and the truant officer has had no obstinate cases brought to his attention.

In the Hgih school there are at present 51 members, divided among courses as follows: College course, 17; English course, 10; and Domestic Arts course 24. The course in Domestic Arts continues to be popular, as all of the girls but six are enrolled in it.

Such text books and supplies as have been needed have been purchased. All classes are well supplied with the necessary reference books.

The usual number of tuition pupils are enrolled and serve as a source of revenue to the district. It is hoped to make their number even larger by legitimate canvassing among the surrounding towns.

Visitors to both the High school and the grades are cordially welcome. It is highly desirable that their number should constantly increase.

The grammar school building is in very good condition, thanks to recent expenditures. In the High school building, however, it should appear desirable to improve the appearance of the walls, and especially to do something towards obtaining slate blackboards, to replace the present substitutes, which have outlasted their period of usefulness.

The teachers at present in the employ of the district are:

In the High school—F. W. Knight, Science and Mathematics; Miss Florence Hubbard, English and Domestic Arts; Miss Emelyn Nickerson, French, Latin and History.

In the grades—Anna Lawrence, grade 8; Emily Cook, grade 7; Ida Mann, grade 6; Caro Clay, grade 5; Minnie Thompson, grade 4; Blanche Rogers, grade 3; Mildred Smith, grade 2; and Mary Roberts, grade 1.

———

As required by law, we herewith submit the following estimates for the next year:

For text books, supplies and appurtenances, $1,000 00

For payment of district notes and interest, $1,400 00

OUTLINE OF STUDY—HIGH SCHOOL.

First Year.

English 1.—Composition and Rhetoric (Scott and Denney). At least thirty themes a year. For reading and study: The Rime of the Ancient Mariner, Silas Marner, Vision of Sir Launfal, Merchant of Venice, Marmion. Eight books read outside of class. Reference books.

Latin 1.—Essentials of Latin (Pearson) complete. First Steps in Latin, (Ritchie) complete. Sight reading.

Ancient History.—West's Ancient World (complete). Greece and Rome to 800 A. D. Constant map work at board. 25 maps per pupil. Outside reading, 400 pages per pupil. Written reports weekly.

Algebra.—Collins' Practical First Year studied through quadratics.

Book-beeping.—William and Roger's Text complete. Drill in preparing business papers and forms. Study of cash book, sales book, journal, ledger and trial balance.

Domestic Arts 1.—Cooking and Sewing. Requirements: to serve at least nine meals a year. Each pupil to serve at least one complete breakfast and luncheon. Study of cooking appliances. Use of kitchen utensils and appliances. Care, setting and serving of table. Designing of menus, study of costs and of nutritive values.

Sewing.—Hand work, machine work, use of patterns, cutting, fitting; making of garments. Study of goods, costs and adaptability to persons. Each pupil to make: apron, corset cover, drawers, nightgown,

11

middy blouse, summer dress or skirt, and to draft a pattern for skirt, shirt waist, drawers and petticoat.

Second Year.

English 2.—Composition, Rhetoric and Literature (Shackford Judson) Thirty themes per year. For reading and study: Washington's Farewell Address, Romeo and Juliet, Golden Treasury, Tale of Two Cities. Eight books read outside class.

Latin 2.—Caesar (Allen and Greenough) four books. Prose composition (Baker Inglis). A term of Ovid. Sight reading.

French 1.—Grammar (New Chardenal) complete. 250 to 300 pages of easy prose. Aldrich & Foster's French Reader.

Geometry.—Text Hart & Feldman's, complete, including from 350 to 450 original exercises.

Arithmetic.—Text, Moore & Miner's, complete. Special emphasis laid on business arithmetic.

Domestic Arts 2.—Household Mechanical Appliances. Study of appliances used inside and around the home, as heating appliances, plumbing, electricity, and other forms of lighting, machines, etc.

Sanitation: applied to the household and surroundings: study of disease, modes of infections, etc. Ventilation, water supply, food supply, disposal of refuse. Study of home site, building plans, treatment of floor, walls, furnishings, and care of same.

Hygiene.—Personal hygiene, care of body, clothing, bedrooms, etc.

English 3.—Composition and Rhetoric (Hitchcock). Thirty themes. Long's English Literature. For Reading and study: Macbeth, Vicar of Wakefield, Webster's First Bunker Hill Oration, Sohrab and Rustum, Carlyle's Essay on Burns. Eight books read outside of class.

Latin 3.—Cicero (D'Ooge) seven orations. Prose Composition (Baker and Inglis). Sight reading.

French 2.—Grammar review. Composition (Francois' Elementary and Advanced Prose). Theme writing (Book review of each book read). Reading 400 to 600 pages of prose. La Belle Nirvernaise, La Mare au Diable L'Abbe Constantin, Colomba.

Physics.—Study of approved manuals, recitations, lectures, laboratory work, etc., experiments are worked out individually with note book results and records.

Rev. Math.—A review and continuation of geometry and algebra.

Domestic Arts.—Physiology (Hough &Sedgwick) References. Laboratory work. Nursing: First aid, care of minor injuries, of the sick, diet for sick, etc. References, charts.

Fourth Year.

English 4.—Composition and Rhetoric (Hitchcock). Thirty themes. Eight outside reading books. Long's American Literature. For reading and study: Romeo and Juliet, Golden Treasury, Tale of Two Cities, Washington's Farewell Address.

Latin 4·—Virgil (Fairclough & Brown). Sight reading. Grammar review and prose work.

French 3.—Prose Composition, (Koren). Parts 1, 2, 3, entire. Book reviews and letter writing. Reading 600 to 900 pages of prose. L'Avare, Huit Contes Choisis, Stories from French Realists, Les Miserables, Eugenie Granget, Le Cid.

Math. Rev. As for third year.

Adv. Math. Solid Geometry, and either Trigonometry or advanced Algebra.

Chemistry.—Recitations, lectures and laboratory work, including 60 or more experiments by individual students with notebook records.

American History.—Essentials in American History (Hart). Essentials of Civil Government (Peterman). Advanced Civics (Forman). Constitution of N. H. and the U. S. A study of the history and government to the present day.

Domestic Arts 4.—An advanced course in cooking, a study of household accounts and marketing. Study of the construction, design, and decoration of the home.

See next page for yearly program of High School.

Respectfully submitted,

ELLIS G. GAMMONS,
ORA A. BROWN,
FREDERICK M. MERROW,
HARRY R. SPAULDING,
EDWARD P. COLBY,
LESTER G. FIFIELD,

Board of Education.

PROGRAM OF ASHLAND HIGH SCHOOL, 1916=17.

Approved July, 1916.

Year	Curriculum I. Latin Course.	Periods per week	Extent	Curriculum II. English Course.	Periods per week	Extent		Periods per week	Extent
I.	Latin Ancient History English Algebra	5 5 5 5	Year " " "	English Ancient History Algebra Book-keeping	5 5 5 5	Year " " "	English Ancient History Algebra Cooking and Sewing	5 5 5 5	Year " " "
II.	Latin Geometry English French	5 5 5 5	Year " " "	English Geometry Arithmetic French	5 5 5 5	Year " " "	English Arithmetic French Mechanical Appliances } Sanitation and Hygiene }	5 5 5 5	Year " " "
III.	Latin English Physics or Chemistry French	5 5 5 5	Year " " "	English Physics or Chemistry Rev. Mathematics French	5 5 5 5	Year " " "	English French Physics or Chemistry Physiology and Nursing	5 5 5 5	Year " " "
IV.	English Latin Rev. Mathematics Am. Const. Hist French	4 4 4 4 4	Year " " "	English French Physics or Chemistry Adv. Mathematics Am. Const. Hist.	4 4 4 4	Year " " "	English Physics or Chemistry Am. Const. Hist French Adv. Cooking and Household	4 4 4 4	Year " " "

SCHOOL TREASURER'S REPORT.

Receipts.

Balance from last year,	$ 233 00
Received from town treasurer,	985 39
Tuition from Holderness,	12 00
Tuition from Harry Leavitt,	7 00
Tuition from Morton Elliott,	4 50
	$1,241 89

Expenditures.

1916

Mar.	1, W. B. Smith, transportation,	$ 25 00
	2, B. M. Warren, teaching,	133 20
	18, E. B. Smith, Calley lease and supplies,	6 25
	23, Addie E. Batchelder, auditor,	2 50
Apr.	7, W. B. Smith, supplies and cleaning school houses,	4 22
	E. B. Smith, supplies,	7 15
	Gladys Smith, transportation,	7 00
May	1, E. B. Smith, wood and bills paid,	11 75
	9, W. B. Smith, transportation,	10 50
June	15, D. S. Batchelder, bills paid,	24 32
	17, George Lambert, transportation,	33 00
	20, B. M. Warren, teaching,	132 00
	W. B. Smith, transportation,	24 50
	E. B. Smith, bills paid,	11 06
	21, O. A. Brown, tuition for Catherine Plummer,	13 33

		O. A. Brown, tuition for Florence Lambert,	13 20
July	5,	Madge Pease, teaching and supplies,	146 72
	7,	O. A. Brown, tuition for Catherine Plummer,	13 34
Aug.	5,	George Lambert, transportation,	12 00
	7,	Plymouth School Dist., tuition for ˴Gladys Smith,	20 00
Oct.	7,	D. S. Batchelder, wood and supplies,	12 14
Nov.	8,	Madge Pease, teaching and supplies,	93 25
		A. J. Smith, transportation,	30 00
	28,	B. M. Warren, teaching 12 weeks,	132 00
Dec.	15,	Howard Small, supplies,	30
	16,	W. B. Smith, transportation,	18 75
	23,	Plymouth School District, tuition for Gladys Smith,	20 00
	25,	Mary J. Chase, transportation,	18 00
	27,	O. A. Brown, tuition for Catherine Plummer,	13 33
1917.			
Jan.	1,	Madge Pease, teaching 8 9-10 weeks,	89 00
		Madge Pease, services as clerk,	2 50
	16,	Leonard Tatham, janitor,	3 00
Feb.	14,	Cash on hand,	158 58

$1,241 89

Respectfully submitted,

B. F. PEASE, Treasurer.

I hereby certify that I have carefully examined the foregoing account of B. F. Pease, treasurer of the town school district, and find it correctly cast and properly vouched.

NELLIE B. CALLEY,

Auditor Town School District.

Feb. 14, 1917.

REPORT OF SCHOOL BOARD.

PEASE DISTRICT.

Fall term, 1915, taught by Miss Madge Pease. Length of term 11 weeks; wages per month, $40.00; whole number of pupils 5; average daily attendance 4.54. Roll of honor, Ethel M. Thompson; George A. Thompson, Hazel Thompson.

Winter term, 1915, taught by Miss Madge Pease. Length of term, 4 2-5 weeks; wages per month, $40.00; whole number of pupils 4; average daily attendance 3.95. Roll of honor, Howard A. Small, George A. Thompson, Ethel M. Thompson.

Spring term, 1916, taught by Miss Madge Pease. Length of term, 14 3-5 weeks; total for year, 30 weeks; wages per month, $40.00; whole number of pupils 6; average daily attendance 5.45. Roll of honor, Guy L. Leavitt, Howard A. Small.

Number of visitors for year, 44.

CALLEY DISTRICT.

Fall term, 1915, taught by Miss Beatrice M. Warren. Length of term 12 weeks; wages per month, $44.00; whole number of pupils 6; average daily attendance 5.80.

Winter term, 1915, taught by Miss Beatrice M. Warren. Length of term 12 weeks; wages per month, $44.00; whole number of pupils 6; average daily attendance 5.52.

Spring term, 1916, taught by Miss Beatrice M. Warren. Length of term 12 weeks; total for year, 36 weeks; wages per month, $44.00; whole number of pupils 7; average daily attendance 5.69.

Number of visitors for year, 27.

———

As Miss Pease and Miss Warren are still in charge of the schools, it shows the high regard in which they are held as teachers.

As it was impossible to get any help, no repairing was done, only some paint and stain purchased.

Owing to the small number of children in the district, the school question is a serious problem.

We would urge all parents and friends to visit the schools as often as possible and see for yourself what the children are receiving from the district schools, and continually impress upon the children the need of an education.

Every voter in the district is urged to attend the annual school meeting, March 17, at 2 p. m., at Ashland Town Hall.

———

As required by law, we submit the following estimates for next year:

For text books, supplies, and appurtenances, $50 00

For High school tuition, $150 00

CHARLES L. SMALL,
ERVILLE J. BATCHELDER,
EVERETT B. SMITH,
School Board.

By Erville J. Batchelder, Chairman.

CPSIA information can be obtained
at www.ICGtesting.com
Printed in the USA
BVHW041031210219
540828BV00009B/328/P